Purple Ronnie's
Little Book for a
Smashing
DAD

by Purple Ronnie

Based on and adapted from the work entitled Purple Ronnie's Little Book for
a Smashing Dad first published in the United Kingdom in 2006 by Pan Macmillan
Publishers Ltd.

08 09 10 11 12 TEN 10 9 8 7 6 5 4 3 2 1

ISBN-13: 978-0-7407-7118-7
ISBN-10: 0-7407-7118-3

Library of Congress Control Number: 2007934068

coolabi.

"Purple Ronnie" created by Giles Andreae. The right of Giles Andreae and Janet
Cronin to be identified respectively as the author and illustrator of this work
has been asserted by them in accordance with the Copyright, Designs, and Patents
Act 1988. This edition of Purple Ronnie's Little Book for a Smashing Dad is
published by arrangement with Purple Enterprises Limited, a Coolabi company.

www.andrewsmcmeel.com

whose kids are these?
much too early
jump
groan
hee hee
bounce
frrp
wriggle
scamper

Remember

All dads deserve to sleep in
just once in a while

Rules of Being a Dad - N°1

You must always have a go at fixing things even if you've got no idea what you're doing

complete rubbish
the flange socket has definitely come out of the gasket trembler
oh no!
TOOLS
gush

☆ Special Tip

Sometimes the smallest room in the house is a dad's best hiding place

The great thing about being a dad is that you get to be in charge of the remote control

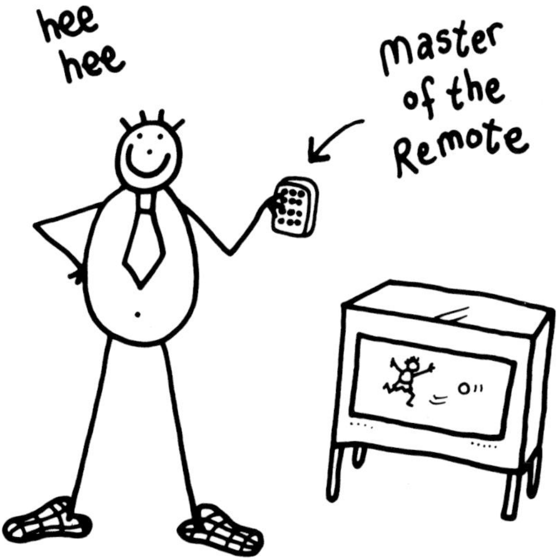
hee
hee
Master
of the
Remote

BANK OF DAD
...one at a time
dinner money please
ballet lessons please
candy please
open all hours

Rules of Being a Dad - N° 2

Your wallet is really just a cash machine for your children

Interesting Fact

Dads' tummies almost always get bigger after they have had children

It's so I can see what you must have gone through, my darling
great big belly
hrumph

Dads and the Newspaper

When dads read the newspaper, it is hardly ever the news that they are really looking at

Rules of Being a Dad - N°3

Never attempt to be trendy.
Old shorts with holes
are usually best

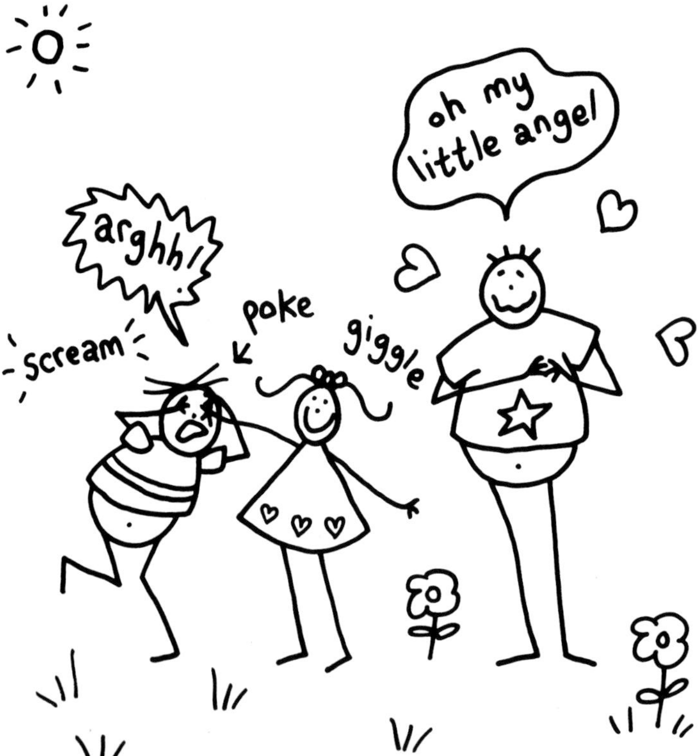

oh my little angel
arghh!
scream
poke
giggle

Dads and their Daughters

Sometimes it can be hard for daddy's little girl to do anything wrong at all

☆ Special Tip

Just once in a while it is nice to let your dad win at football

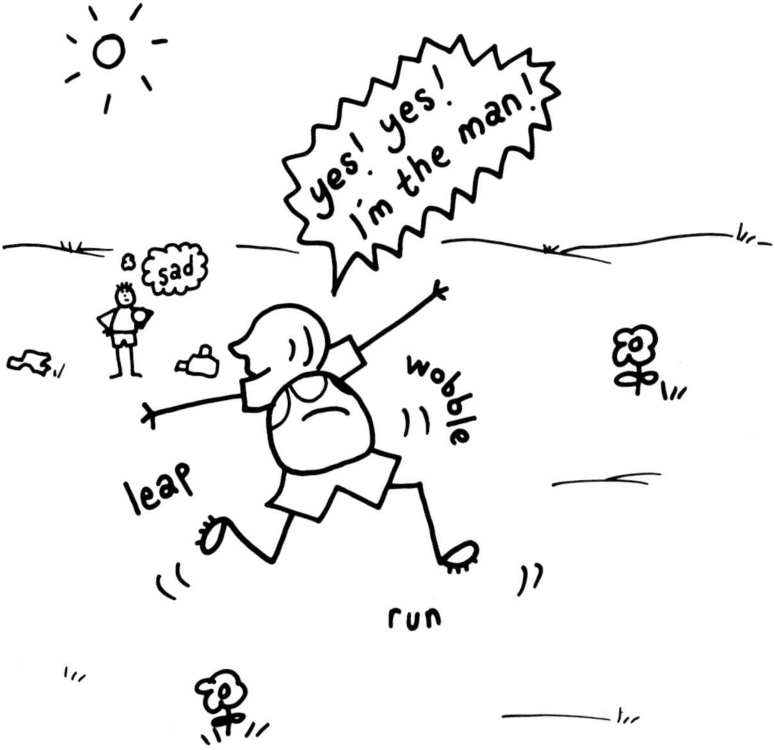
yes! yes! i'm the man!
sad
wobble
leap
run

Rules of Being a Dad - Nº 4

If it's your house, you can fart wherever you like

Sometimes, all a dad needs
at the end of the day is
a nice big drink

Dads and the Telephone

To most dads the telephone
is the enemy

Rules of Being a Dad - N° 5

Your car is a taxi and you are the unpaid driver

Warning

Some dads just aren't
made for DIY

Rules of Being a Dad - Nº 6

Dads don't get letters.
Dads just get bills

Some dads are never happier than when they're puttering in the garden

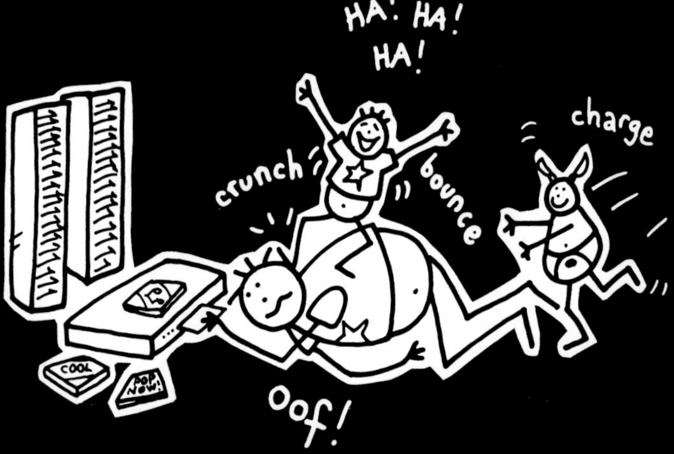

HA! HA!
HA!
charge
crunch
bounce
COOL
POP NOW!
oof!

Warning

To little children, a dad is sometimes just a great big jungle gym

Rules of Being a Dad - N°7

When you've got your slippers on, the world becomes a better place

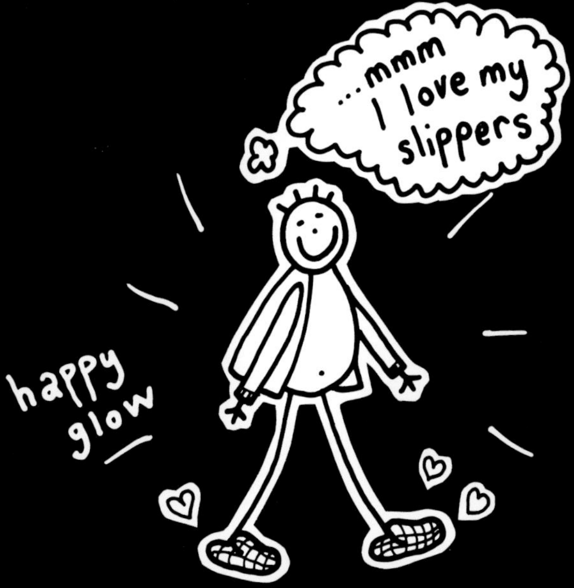
...mmm I love my slippers
happy glow

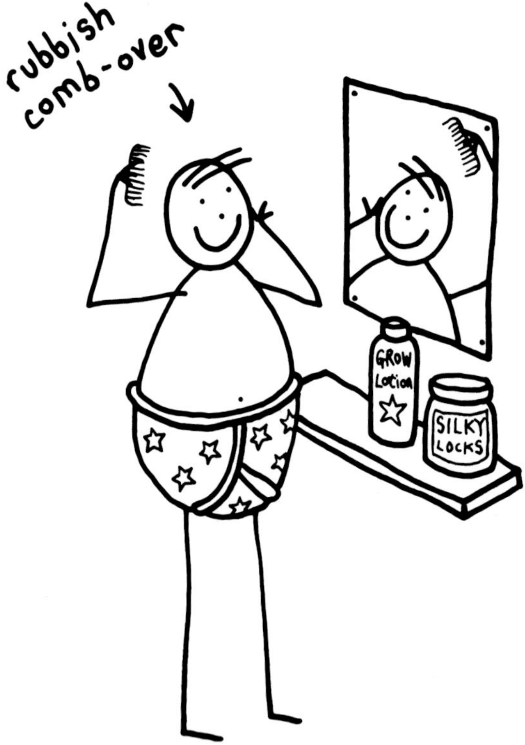
rubbish comb-over
GROW Lotion
SILKY LOCKS

Some dads will do anything to make it look like they've still got loads of hair

☆ <u>Special Tip</u>

There are some jobs that only a dad can do

Rules of Being a Dad - Nº 8

Never _ever_ dance in front of your children

Dads can be very useful in all sorts of difficult situations

um, can I have my son's ball back please...
scary boys
gulp
v. brave
shake
DIE

Dads' Fantasies

When you become a dad, your favorite fantasies start to change

Rules of Being a Dad - No9

You are completely in charge of directions wherever you go

☆ Special Tip

Moms have special ways of getting dads to do things for them

Warning

No one else even thinks about sitting in dad's favorite armchair

invisible force field

T.V. remotes

Rules of Being a Dad - Nº 10

However much stuff there is to carry, you are the only one who has to carry it

☆ **Special Tip**

Sometimes, all a dad needs to be happy is a little bit of peace and quiet